Change and Continuity in Crime in Rural America

by Ralph A. Weisheit and Joseph F. Donnermeyer

The study of rural crime has the potential to make important contributions to crime policy, criminological theory, and research methods in criminology. Although most places in America remain rural, researchers have paid insufficient attention to rural crime and have not utilized the wide variations among rural areas as natural laboratories for research. This chapter outlines what is known about rural crime and suggests likely rural crime issues for the future. Understanding rural crime requires understanding factors that make rural life distinct from urban life, including geography and culture. Understanding rural crime and anticipating future rural crime issues also requires understanding how technology, economic factors, and demographics shape the nature of rural crime. Official police data and victimization data are used to examine the levels of rural crime and to compare patterns of rural and urban crime. A variety of sources are used to examine substance abuse and domestic violence, two types of crime that appear to have similar rates across rural and urban areas. The chapter also focuses on the emerging issue of environmental crime in rural areas. And, despite the importance of race in urban studies of crime, little rural crime research has directly addressed links between race and crime.

Dr. Ralph A. Weisheit is a Professor in the Department of Criminal Justice, Illinois State University in Normal. Dr. Joseph F. Donnermeyer is a Professor in the Department of Human and Community Resources Development at The Ohio State University in Columbus.

Two popular yet seemingly contradictory images of American society persist. In one the world is shrinking. The rapid movement of people and goods through the emergence of a world economy, combined with nearly instantaneous communication, has allowed for an unprecedented exchange of cultural ideas across long distances. Fast food chains, franchise stores, television, the Internet, and improved transportation have led to the homogenization or "massification" of American culture (e.g., Fischer 1980). The idea that America has become a mass society, combined with population growth and a highly mobile population, suggests that "rural" is vanishing in both spacial and cultural terms.

A second view sees an American society of growing diversity. Ironically, diversity is stimulated by three of the forces cited in support of the mass society view: the global economy, improved transportation, and worldwide communication, each of which continuously brings new people, ideas, and products into the country.

Rural culture survives and thrives in many areas of the United States, despite the forces of massification and diversity. To make the concept of rural useful to criminology, rural places must be viewed as a diverse array of people, places, and cultures that present rich opportunities for contemporary research on crime and the advancement of criminological theory.

There are more than 65 million rural citizens in the United States, though estimates vary depending on which definition of rural is used. This represents approximately one-fourth of the country's population, more than any single minority group in America and larger than most countries. For example, the total populations of Great Britain and France are about 59 million each, and Italy is home to approximately 58 million people. Rural places account for about 70 percent of the land mass of the United States. And, although most people in the United States live in urban areas, most places are rural.

The concept of rural is also of theoretical importance, particularly for theories using concepts of place and physical space (see Weisheit and Wells 1996). Theories that cannot account for both rural and urban circumstances are *limited in scope*; they may be only theories of urban crime. Furthermore, because there are many more rural places than urban places, and given that the rural places display an incredible variety of cultural, economic, and social conditions, theories that do not account for variation in structural conditions of rural (and urban) places lack generalizability. This is a particular problem if they are treated as general theories by policymakers.

Urban-based explanations of crime are also inadequate if they are based on faulty assumptions about
factors associated with crime. For example, the
assumption that the availability of guns fuels high
crime rates is inconsistent with the experience of
rural areas, in which gun ownership is common and
yet guns are *less often* used in homicides, rapes, or
robberies than in the largest cities (Weisheit, Falcone,
and Wells 1999). Including rural settings in an analysis of the role of guns in crime requires a different
and substantially more complex explanatory framework for understanding the relationship between guns
and crime.

> *Theories that cannot account for both rural and urban circumstances are limited in scope; they may be only theories of urban crime.*

What Is Rural?

As a concept, rural defies simple definition. The term has been used to describe
unincorporated areas, villages, small towns, townships, counties, States, and
even countries. It is sometimes used to describe a geographic area, while at
other times it refers to a culture or worldview. In other circumstances, the term
refers to areas in which the local economy is based on agriculture, mining, logging, and other extractive industries, and some rural tourist communities may
have small permanent populations that swell to urban proportions during tourist
season.

The broad use of the term rural is also common in research. Most studies of
rural crime do not provide an operational definition of the term rural (Weisheit,
Falcone, and Wells 1999). In fact, there is no single simple definition that cap-
tures the essence of rural, is quantifiable, and is applicable to a variety of rural
settings. This chapter reflects the various ways in which the term rural has been
employed. The most commonly used operational definitions of rural come from
the U.S. Bureau of the Census. For example, for some county-level data the
Census Bureau's metropolitan/nonmetropolitan dichotomy provides a crude
but serviceable empirical indicator of rural; when discussing community-level
issues, the Census Bureau's practice of treating unincorporated areas and towns
with less than 2,500 residents as rural is also useful, if imprecise. More recently, places in America have been classified into taxonomies representing a con-
tinuum of places from the least to the most densely populated. One example
is the U.S. Department of Agriculture's classification of all nonmetropolitan
counties into categories based on population size and distance to the nearest
metropolitan county. All census-based definitions thus represent rough guides
for distinguishing rural from urban.

Another problem with discussing rural crime and culture is the extreme diversity in social, economic, and political conditions across different rural settings. For example, rural Wyoming is very different from rural Delaware in a number of dimensions, including population density, proximity to urban places, composition of the population, and economic base. Thus, wide variations in the cultural, economic, and social conditions of rural (and urban) communities suggest that some rural and urban differences may be situationally specific. The challenge is to capture the essence of rural while also appreciating wide variations among rural areas. When we focus on future trends, our intention is to emphasize broad national and regional patterns that will have direct implications for local problems and local responses.

General Patterns of Rural Crime

There are two stereotypes about rural crime in America. One image is of a bucolic countryside where crime is rare. This stereotype is reflected in television programs such as "The Andy Griffith Show," in which violent crime is practically unknown. Another image is of serious violent crime perpetrated by "rednecks" or "white trash." These individuals, as portrayed in films such as "Deliverance" and "Sling Blade," are amoral, revengeful, and violent. Neither stereotype holds up well under scrutiny. Rural crime does generally occur less frequently than urban crime, but there are important exceptions. Furthermore, there are substantial variations among rural areas in geography, economics, demography, and culture. Consequently, there are wide variations in the levels and forms of crime in rural America. There are, for example, rural pockets with extreme violence and high homicide rates (cf. Angle 1980; Montell 1986), although in general rural homicide rates are much lower than urban rates. Here it is possible only to examine general urban-rural differences. We begin with two national sources of data: the Federal Bureau of Investigation's (FBI's) Uniform Crime Reports (UCR) data and the National Crime Victimization Survey (NCVS).

The belief that crime occurs less frequently in rural areas is supported by recent UCR data (see exhibit 1). Of particular interest is a comparison between police reports of crime in cities of 250,000 people or more and in rural counties that are outside metropolitan statistical areas and cover areas not under the jurisdiction of municipal police departments. Exhibit 1 shows that urban crime rates are higher than rural crime rates for every FBI Crime Index offense. Violent crime rates are especially high in large cities relative to rural counties. The greatest difference is for robbery, which occurs more than 26 times more often in urban areas. In general, the types of crime that are most frequent in large

Exhibit 1. Crime rates (per 100,000) for cities of 250,000 or more versus rural counties, 1997

Crime type	Cities 250,000+	Rural counties	City:rural ratio
Violent crime			
Total	1,358.5	251.5	5.4:1
Murder	16.1	4.5	3.6:1
Rape	54.2	25.8	2.1:1
Robbery	533.1	20.5	26.0:1
Aggravated assault	755.2	200.7	3.8:1
Property crime			
Total	6,357.5	2,055.3	3.1:1
Burglary	1,295.5	697.4	1.9:1
Larceny	3,928.9	1,214.3	3.2:1
Vehicle theft	1,133.1	143.6	7.9:1
Arson*	77.8	17.8	4.4:1

* The figures for arson are drawn from table 2.31 of UCR and are not included in the row on total property crime.

Source: U.S. Department of Justice, Federal Bureau of Investigation 1998, table 16.

cities are also those that are most frequent in rural areas, with the exception of robbery, which is overwhelmingly an urban crime.

Official counts of crime are useful indicators, but they suffer from a number of shortcomings. Not all crimes are reported to authorities, not all reported crimes are recorded, and not all recorded crimes are forwarded to the FBI's UCR. One alternative is to ask citizens whether they have been victims of crime. NCVS is an annual survey begun in 1973 that uses a randomly drawn national sample and includes information about the size of the respondent's community. The 1990 survey, for example, reported the percentage of households indicating any form of victimization in urban, suburban, and rural areas was 30 percent, 23 percent, and 17 percent, respectively. Bachman (1992a, 1992b) noted that between 1973 and 1990 victimization was consistently highest in central cities and lowest in nonmetropolitan areas.

A few studies have analyzed crime variations among rural areas (e.g., Donnermeyer and Phillips 1982; Miller, Hoiberg, and Ganey 1982; Smith and Huff 1982), generally focusing on patterns across rural areas and correlates of rural crime. Arthur

(1991), for example, examined property and violent crime in 13 rural Georgia counties. He found that unemployment, poverty, public aid, and race were related to both property and violent crime rates; relationships were particularly strong for property crime. Bankston and Allen (1980) compared homicides among 10 social areas in rural Louisiana and found that both socioeconomic and cultural factors shaped homicide rates. Significantly, the relative importance of each varied from one social area to another, suggesting the importance of appreciating variations among rural areas.

Trends in rural crime

An important aspect of anticipating future rural crime patterns is looking at patterns in the recent past. Concern that rural and urban crime rates are converging has raised considerable debate. Exhibit 2 uses UCR data from 1966 through 1997 to compare rural-urban rates over time for both violent and property offenses, and exhibit 3 plots the city to rural crime ratio based on these data. Several things in these exhibits are worth noting. First, violent crime in large cities rose from 1966 through 1991 and then declined, while rural rates drifted upward for the entire period. However, any convergence between urban and rural rates was modest. Between 1991 and 1997, urban rates of violence declined by 531.8 per 100,000 people, while rural rates increased by 37.9 per 100,000. Urban and rural rates were closest in 1997, but violent Index offenses were still five times more frequent in the largest cities and were more the result of declines in urban violence than increases in rural violence. Second, property crime fluctuated over time in both large cities and rural areas, but the overall gap between rural and urban property crime rates changed much less over time than it did for violent crime.

Exhibits 2 and 3 do not cover crimes outside of the seven Index categories. Some offenses, such as youth gang activity, may be of particular concern as emerging issues in rural areas. Non-Index offenses are not reported in UCR by population density, so these comparisons are not possible from published results. Other rural-specific offenses, such as rustling and the theft of grain or farm machinery, are not separated from general crime categories. Exhibit 4 shows that changes are not the same for all offenses. Between 1966 and 1997, rural murder rates changed little, but robbery, burglary, and motor vehicle theft doubled, and rape, aggravated assault, and larceny either tripled or nearly tripled. Among violent crimes, murder changed relatively little over time while rape and aggravated assault both increased. Robbery increased from 1966 through 1974, declined from 1983 through 1990, and then increased between 1990 and 1997. Among property crimes, burglaries increased between 1966 and 1980 and declined between 1980 and 1983, but did not change dramatically after that. Larceny increased between 1966 and 1980, but showed no clear

Exhibit 2. Crime rates for cities of 250,000 or more versus rural counties, 1966–97

	Violent crime			Property crime		
Year	Cities 250,000+*	Rural counties*	City:rural ratio	Cities 250,000+*	Rural counties*	City:rural ratio
1966	505.1	84.5	6.0:1	4,044.0	841.0	4.8:1
1967	626.4	93.0	6.7:1	3,162.5	690.0	4.6:1
1968	773.2	96.5	8.0:1	3,680.2	782.2	4.7:1
1969	859.7	102.9	8.4:1	3,965.0	860.2	4.6:1
1970	980.4	101.9	9.6:1	4,354.7	882.8	4.9:1
1971	1,047.5	115.7	9.1:1	4,366.0	984.0	4.4:1
1972	998.6	128.2	7.8:1	3,949.3	1,026.1	3.8:1
1973	1,003.4	134.0	7.5:1	5,579.5	1,400.2	4.0:1
1974	1,107.9	161.6	6.9:1	6,390.9	1,849.8	3.5:1
1975	1,158.9	176.8	6.6:1	7,043.7	2,052.2	3.4:1
1976	1,095.4	174.2	6.3:1	7,167.1	2,040.7	3.5:1
1977	1,070.4	175.5	6.1:1	6,748.6	1,909.2	3.5:1
1978	1,120.8	185.4	6.1:1	6,760.2	1,950.1	3.5:1
1979	1,237.8	194.0	6.4:1	7,218.1	2,076.1	3.5:1
1980	1,414.2	185.9	7.6:1	7,987.9	2,215.8	3.6:1
1981	1,440.9	179.4	8.0:1	8,030.4	2,119.1	3.8:1
1982	1,353.9	184.2	7.4:1	7,851.0	2,041.2	3.9:1
1983	1,294.0	165.0	7.8:1	7,345.4	1,824.8	4.0:1
1984	1,288.3	159.8	8.1:1	7,307.5	1,740.5	4.2:1
1985	1,344.5	176.9	7.6:1	7,606.1	1,743.8	4.4:1
1986	1,645.5	192.8	8.5:1	7,993.8	1,791.1	4.5:1
1987	1,603.8	193.9	8.3:1	8,062.7	1,887.5	4.3:1
1988	1,540.4	180.7	8.5:1	8,271.3	1,882.3	4.4:1
1989	1,641.1	198.2	8.3:1	8,425.0	1,923.3	4.4:1
1990	1,813.0	209.0	8.7:1	8,361.4	1,923.1	4.4:1
1991	1,890.3	213.6	8.9:1	8,223.0	1,978.0	4.2:1
1992	1,802.1	226.2	8.0:1	7,722.2	1,927.6	4.0:1
1993	1,711.9	233.1	7.3:1	7,492.6	1,883.3	4.0:1
1994	1,657.4	255.9	6.5:1	7,129.0	1,936.5	3.7:1
1995	1,564.3	253.0	6.2:1	6,998.9	2,011.8	3.5:1
1996	1,443.7	242.6	6.0:1	6,647.2	2,014.8	3.3:1
1997	1,358.5	251.5	5.4:1	6,357.5	2,055.3	3.1:1

* Numbers represent the rate of crimes reported per 100,000 people.

Source: U.S. Department of Justice, Federal Bureau of Investigation 1960–97 (see exhibit 1).

Exhibit 3. Ratio of city to rural crime, 1966–97

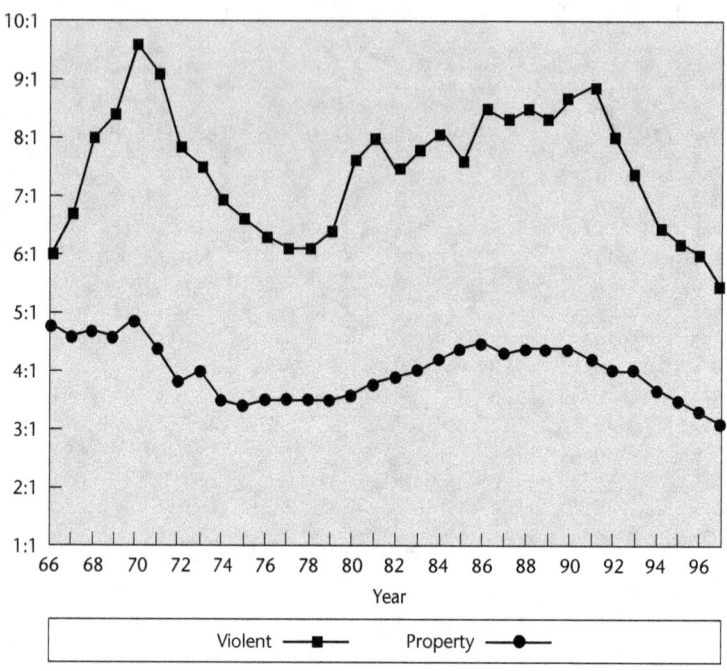

Source: Based on data presented in exhibit 2, columns 3 and 6.

pattern after that. Motor vehicle theft increased from 1966 through 1980, declined from 1980 through 1985, and then rose from 1985 through 1997.

NCVS also permits considering changes over time by community size and provides an alternative data source in which changes in official recordkeeping are not an issue. Exhibit 5 shows that rural violent victimization is persistently lower than urban violent victimization. Where convergence has occurred, it is between suburban and rural areas. This has more to do with drops in suburban victimization than with increases in rural victimization. Rural crime changed less over time than either suburban or urban crime, with all three showing declines in the most recent years.

Fischer (1980) used data on violent crime in selected California counties to argue that changes in urban counties were followed by changes in rural counties, with crime diffusing first to smaller cities and then to the rural hinterland. This

Exhibit 4. Offense-specific Index crime rates for rural counties, 1966–97

Year	Violent crime				Property crime		
	Murder	Rape	Robbery	Assault	Burglary	Larceny	Motor vehicle theft
1966	4.7	8.9	10.0	60.9	335.1	445.2	60.7
1967	5.0	9.2	11.5	67.2	403.7	509.3	67.7
1968	5.3	9.7	12.9	68.6	454.6	543.1	75.2
1969	4.9	10.6	13.4	73.9	476.8	595.2	84.4
1970	5.5	9.5	13.3	73.6	477.2	606.1	80.3
1971	5.9	10.7	14.5	84.6	531.6	657.5	76.8
1972	6.2	10.9	16.1	94.9	558.1	667.2	72.5
1973	6.5	11.9	16.7	98.9	594.4	721.2	84.6
1974	7.8	13.1	22.7	118.0	791.6	955.8	102.5
1975	8.4	13.2	24.9	130.4	872.6	1,068.7	110.9
1976	7.5	13.3	20.7	132.6	825.5	1,103.1	112.2
1977	7.9	14.4	20.8	132.4	788.6	999.3	121.2
1978	7.9	14.9	21.4	141.2	795.9	1,021.2	133.0
1979	7.6	15.6	22.8	148.1	803.0	1,130.0	143.1
1980	7.4	16.0	23.0	139.5	871.8	1,202.6	141.4
1981	7.0	15.7	22.1	134.6	836.7	1,157.7	124.7
1982	6.8	15.4	20.4	141.6	788.3	1,132.9	119.9
1983	5.8	15.3	16.9	127.0	693.7	1,027.6	103.6
1984	5.2	17.5	14.9	122.3	651.3	987.1	102.2
1985	5.6	18.5	15.0	137.7	668.2	967.2	108.4
1986	5.4	20.1	15.6	145.4	697.7	978.4	115.1
1987	5.7	19.6	15.6	146.7	728.1	1,040.9	118.5
1988	5.4	19.6	14.8	140.9	711.1	1,051.8	119.4
1989	5.4	22.8	16.4	153.6	719.9	1,077.4	126.0
1990	5.7	23.7	15.8	163.8	708.1	1,087.6	127.4
1991	5.6	25.4	17.0	165.6	741.0	1,114.0	123.0
1992	5.3	27.3	17.0	176.7	701.4	1,109.6	116.6
1993	5.5	26.6	17.1	183.8	675.5	1,087.3	120.5
1994	5.2	28.4	18.6	203.6	679.9	1,127.7	128.8
1995	5.3	26.2	18.6	203.0	687.4	1,186.6	137.8
1996	4.8	24.6	18.0	195.3	680.0	1,196.5	138.3
1997	4.5	25.8	20.5	200.7	697.4	1,214.3	143.6

Note: Numbers represent the rate of crimes reported per 100,000 people.

Source: U.S. Department of Justice, Federal Bureau of Investigation 1960–97.

argument is consistent with contemporary observations about the rise of gangs in rural areas. Rural gangs are more common in areas adjacent to the largest cities, and even those in more remote rural areas often have ties to gangs in larger communities (Donnermeyer 1994; Weisheit, Falcone, and Wells 1999; Wells and Weisheit 1998). It is not clear which factors facilitate and which hinder this diffusion, or for which types of crime this diffusion process operates.

Our attention now shifts from Index offenses and general crime to several specific offenses. Alcohol, illicit drugs, and domestic violence are general problems in American society. They are also among the crimes for which urban-rural differences are relatively small. Finally, environmental crime is emerging as a serious rural crime issue.

Exhibit 5. Violent victimization, 1973–97

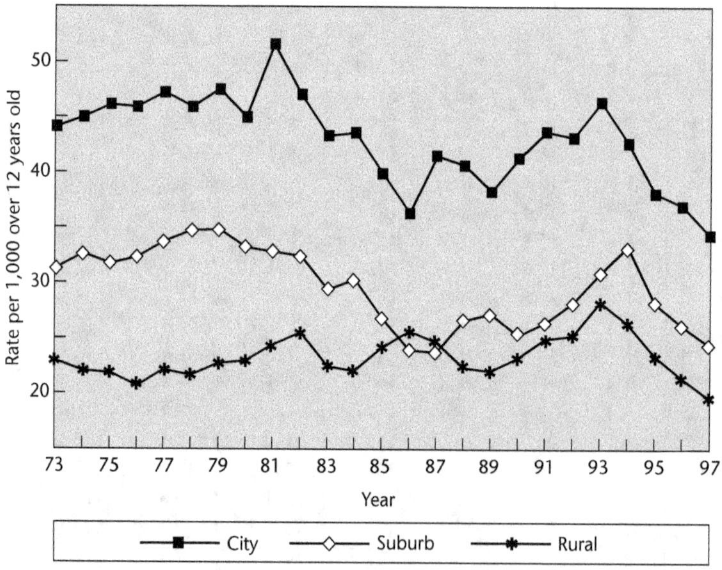

Sources: Thanks to Dr. L. Edward Wells for preparing these data. Because of changes in the instrument, post-1992 rates were adjusted to be comparable to pre-1992 rates. For violent crimes, the multiplier is 0.671 times the post-1993 rates. These data were assembled from a variety of sources, including Bachman 1992a, 1992b; Bastian 1995; Perkins and Klaus 1996; Taylor 1997; Ringel 1997; and Rand, Lynch, and Cantor 1997.

Alcohol and drugs

Rural substance use includes use by rural citizens and criminal trafficking by organizations. The professional literature has discussed the issue of substance use, while the issue of rural trafficking organizations has more often been addressed in the popular press.

Alcohol use is of particular concern in rural areas. Driving under the influence (DUI) for example, is more common in rural areas. According to UCR, the rate of arrest for DUI in cities with fewer than 10,000 residents is more than double that in cities of 250,000 or more, and the rates for both suburban and rural counties are much higher than in the largest cities.

Alcohol remains the drug of choice among American youths, and alcohol use by rural youths has consistently matched or exceeded use by urban youths over more than 20 years of surveying high school seniors.

Alcohol remains the drug of choice among American youths, and alcohol use by rural youths has consistently matched or exceeded use by urban youths over more than 20 years of surveying high school seniors. The Monitoring the Future study (Cronk and Sarvela 1997) reported that about 74 percent of both nonmetropolitan and metropolitan youths said they consumed alcohol in the previous year. However, nonmetropolitan youths were more likely to report getting drunk (56.7 percent versus 51.4 percent in 1995). Even if urban and rural rates of alcohol use by young people were similar, the rural setting may be cause for greater concern:

> Similar rates of alcohol use, however, may be more of a problem for rural than for urban youth because rural youth must spend more time on the roads. The distances that must be traveled from homes to school and other entertainment events, or even to visit friends, are generally much greater for rural youth than for urban youth. The lack of availability of public transportation means that these youth spend a significant amount of time in cars. Most social use of alcohol by these rural teens is followed by driving or at least riding in a car where the driver has been drinking. The relative lack of traffic on rural roadways and the distances to be traversed often lead to driving at high rates of speed. With many rural roads in poor condition, poorly marked for hazards, and poorly lit, these youth are already at higher risk of accidents leading to injury or death. (Peters, Oetting, and Edwards 1992, 25–26)

The Monitoring the Future study also permits comparisons of substance use across urban and rural areas. In 1975, 39 percent of nonmetropolitan seniors had used an illicit substance in the past year, compared with 55 percent of seniors from the largest metropolitan areas and 45 percent from other metropolitan areas. By the peak year of 1979, the rate for nonmetropolitan seniors had risen to 48 percent, compared with 61 percent and 55 percent from the largest metropolitan areas and other metropolitan areas, respectively. By 1992, substance use was 27 percent for all three groups. Thus, urban-rural convergence was due more to a decline in urban rates than to an increase in rural rates. Since 1992, substance use rates have risen more rapidly for metropolitan than for other youths. By 1995, 42 percent of 12th graders from the largest metropolitan counties had tried a substance in the past year, compared with 36 percent of nonmetropolitan youths.

Data from Monitoring the Future also indicate that youths from nonmetropolitan counties were consistently more likely than urban youths to use cigarettes and smokeless tobacco. As for other drugs, nonmetropolitan 12th graders in 1995 had similar rates for past year use of inhalants and powder cocaine, and slightly higher rates for crack cocaine, stimulants, barbiturates, and tranquilizers.

Donnermeyer's (1992) summary and analysis of 65 research locality-specific studies of drug use by rural youths concluded that rural and urban rates were similar. He also noted the relative paucity of research on rural drug issues, in particular the lack of information about how rural youths gain access to drugs.

A 1990 report to Congress by the U.S. General Accounting Office concluded that the rate of total drug use, including alcohol, was similar across rural and urban areas, but there were differences in the types of drugs used. Powder cocaine use was lower in rural areas, but the use of inhalants was higher. Furthermore, although total drug arrest rates were similar across areas, alcohol arrests were higher and drug arrests lower in rural areas.

An indirect way of comparing rural and urban drug use is to use arrest statistics. Belyea and Zingraff (1985) compared drug arrest data in North Carolina for urban and rural counties between 1976 and 1980 and concluded that rural arrest rates were consistently lower and that there was no evidence that rural and urban rates were converging. Castellano and Uchida (1990) estimated that the rate of drug arrests in urban areas was nearly four times that in rural counties. They speculated that because most drug enforcement was proactive, variations in arrest rates among jurisdictions were more the result of differences in enforcement efforts than in consumption patterns.

Rural drug trafficking and production are less well understood than is rural drug use. Although there is a tendency to think that the illegal production of alcohol is a historical curiosity, there are many parts of rural America where illicit alcohol production continues as a lucrative business. In rural Virginia alone, for example, it is estimated that about 500,000 gallons of moonshine are distilled each year, with a street value of $25 or more per gallon (Verde 1998). Similar problems are likely in other rural States, particularly those with a history of moonshining.

Reports suggest that rural areas may serve as production sites for methamphetamine, designer drugs, crack cocaine, and marijuana (Bai 1997; McCormick and O'Donnell 1993; Weisheit 1993, 1992, 1997; Baker et al. 1989; Weingarten 1989; Clayton 1995; Tyson 1996; Howlett 1997; Kirn 1998; Stewart and Sitaramiah 1997). Weisheit's (1993, 1992) studies of commercial marijuana growers found they were almost exclusively rural operations. Regarding methamphetamine laboratories:

> Although an increasing number of these laboratories are confiscated in urban and suburban neighborhoods, the majority are seized in rural sections throughout the country. Because of the chemical odors and toxic wastes associated with the manufacturing process, isolation is often the best defense against detection. Therefore, operators commonly establish their laboratories in sparsely populated areas as a way to conceal their activities while minimizing their risk of discovery. Their operations are typically larger and more sophisticated than laboratories operating in more densely populated communities. (O'Dea, Murphy, and Balzer 1997, 80)

In 1997, the State with the largest number of detected methamphetamine laboratories was Missouri, and most of the laboratories were in rural areas (Stewart and Sitaramiah 1997; Wren 1997).

Other reports argue that rural areas have become important transshipment points for drugs destined for cities (Weingarten and Coates 1989; *Chicago Tribune* 1989). The problem is exacerbated by the improved highway system and by the large number of isolated airstrips set up for corporate farms and crop dusters serving rural farmlands.

Although predicting future patterns of rural substance use and production is difficult, rural drug production will probably become a more serious problem. Opium poppies can easily be grown in rural America. It is unlikely that large-scale production of opium will be possible or economically practical, but there is no reason that small-scale "hobbyists" cannot emerge (cf. Pollan 1997).

Family violence

Although intimate abuse and child abuse have been studied extensively, few studies have focused specifically on rural areas and even fewer have compared urban and rural areas. It appears that rates of abuse are similar across rural and urban areas, but rural areas have fewer resources for responding. In some rural communities, the problem is compounded by a culture that defines family violence as a private matter.

In her observational study of families in a rural Appalachian community, Gagne (1992, 410–412) noted that both the police and the prosecutor were reluctant to act in abuse cases, and as a consequence, women were reluctant to call them for assistance:

> Most people I met agreed that police protection in Raven Ridge was inadequate. John explained that it took at least an hour for an officer to arrive after a call was placed, and that once the cruiser arrived, the officers would sit in the car and beep the horn rather than come to the door. . . . Acceptance of a man's authority over his wife and the belief in the sanctity of the home, together with officers' belief that they would be in danger if they responded to domestic calls, resulted in the failure of the legal system to provide protection for physically battered women.

Concern about officer safety is justified in small rural agencies, in which about 60 percent of domestic violence calls are responded to by a single officer unit for whom backup is often far away (Weisheit, Falcone, and Wells 1999).

Websdale's ethnographic study of battered women in Kentucky (1995, 1998) echoed and expanded upon Gagne's observations. Abuse was facilitated by physical isolation, a patriarchal ideology, and isolation from potentially supportive institutions, including child care, health care, schooling, and other social services. Websdale (1998, 5) states:

> One of the most common complaints of rural battered women concerns the physical and geographical isolation they experience. Some battered women who live up what is locally called a "hollow" (a secluded dirt road cul-de-sac with a small number of houses on it) seem to live extraordinarily isolated lives. Several of the women report not having any friends for years. With no public transportation and large distances between houses, they report that it is often physically difficult to engage in community life.

The involvement of police in these settings is shaped by their integration into the community. Where the officer is related to or friends with the woman, domestic violence laws may be aggressively enforced. More commonly, the officer is acquainted with the male batterer or is sympathetic to the batterer's position:

> Susan reported that nearly the whole community knew that her husband beat her brutally on a regular basis. However, the local police officer in the small town where they lived in Western Kentucky did not offer her any protection. She told me the local constable was her husband's brother and refused to arrest her husband. Susan also noted it was common knowledge that the constable beat his own wife and confronting domestic violence was not part of his "calling" as a law enforcement officer. (Websdale 1998, 103)

> *Most (68 percent) rural agencies report having no shelter for battered women in their jurisdiction, and for those without a shelter, the nearest is an average of 36 miles away.*

Paradoxically, the more detached the police are from the community, the more likely they are to enforce domestic violence laws. Rural women mentioned that State police are more likely to make arrests, remove men from the home as opposed to removing women from the home, and inform battered women of their rights under the law. (Websdale 1998, 123)

The response of rural police to domestic violence may be changing. In our conversations with rural officers, this issue arose frequently, usually reflecting heightened sensitivity to the issue. It is possible that rural police are increasingly willing to intervene in domestic violence cases—both because research suggests that arrest may be an effective deterrent and out of concern for lawsuits that could result from inaction, as a growing number of States have passed legislation mandating a police response and an arrest in domestic violence calls. However, further study is needed to determine if and how the rural police response is shaped by these legislative initiatives and by changes in the way that domestic violence is perceived. More also needs to be known about how community services available in rural areas shape the responses of the criminal justice system. Most (68 percent) rural agencies report having no shelter for battered women in their jurisdiction, and for those without a shelter, the nearest is an average of 36 miles away (Weisheit, Falcone, and Wells 1999).

Even less is known about rural-urban differences in child abuse, but two studies by the National Center on Child Abuse and Neglect (U.S. Department of Health and Human Services 1981, 1988) are suggestive. The first study was conducted in 1980, the second in 1986. In 1980, abuse was defined as "demonstrated harm as a result of maltreatment" (1988, ix), and in this study, abuse rates were higher

> *Impoverished rural areas also may be under great financial pressure to serve as legal dumping sites for urban centers, often for other States.*

in rural areas than in major urban counties. The 1986 study included a definition of abuse that mirrored that of 1980 but also included children "placed at risk for harm," such as by being left alone. In this study, urban rates of abuse were higher. The studies were based on a relatively small number of counties and could not address contextual issues that would explain these differences. Other research suggests that, compared with doctors in larger cities, physicians in small towns detect more child abuse but are *less* likely to report cases to the authorities (Badger 1989).

Another source of information about both spouse abuse and child abuse is the National Family Violence Survey (NFVS). This self-report national survey was first conducted in 1975 (Straus, Gelles, and Steinmetz 1980) and again in 1985 (Straus and Gelles 1990). Both surveys were designed to include substantial numbers of rural respondents.

The 1975 NFVS found that large cities (with a population of 1 million or more) had the highest rates of child abuse, while rural, suburban, and small city rates were similar. The 1985 survey found no differences in child abuse rates across communities of different sizes (Wolfner and Gelles 1993). Regarding spouse abuse, the 1975 survey found that rates were highest in large cities and rural areas, and lowest in small cities and suburbs. However, the differences were rather small. Curiously, although the 1985 study was designed specifically to include urban, suburban, and rural respondents, the major book describing the 1985 findings (Straus and Gelles 1990) made no mention of differences in spouse abuse by community size.

There is no evidence that child abuse or spouse abuse are increasing in rural areas. There does appear to be a heightened sensitivity to domestic violence and a greater willingness by rural authorities to respond. The challenge for the future will be to provide criminal justice and social services resources, particularly in the most impoverished and remote rural areas.

Environmental crime

An emerging rural issue is ecological crime, including both crimes against the environment and crimes committed in the name of the environment. Ecological crimes are of concern in urban areas, but it is in rural America that such crimes are likely to become particularly problematic.

Crimes against the environment

Crimes against the environment include a range of activities, from the illegal dumping of toxic waste to the illegal harvesting of trees. The extent to which rural areas are used to illegally dump hazardous waste is not known, but the isolation of many rural areas makes such dumping relatively easy. As the problem of disposing of hazardous waste grows and the cost of legally disposing of that waste climbs, illegal dumping in rural areas will likely increase, as will the risk to the health and welfare of rural residents.

> *In Federal forests alone, it is estimated that timber theft could total as much as $100 million each year and may account for as many as 1 in 10 trees cut in the National Forest System.*

Impoverished rural areas also may be under great financial pressure to serve as *legal* dumping sites for urban centers, often for other States (*Rachel's Hazardous Waste News #66* 1988). There are thousands of landfills and similar in-ground storage sites that are contaminated and leaking:

> The United States government estimates that over sixteen thousand active landfills have been sopped with industrial and agricultural hazardous wastes. Most are located near small towns and farming communities— and the contents of them, according to the Environmental Protection Agency (EPA), will eventually breach their linings and penetrate the soil, as many already have done. (Setterberg and Shavelson 1993, 4)

A thriving illicit industry is likely to include everything from cleanup scams that defraud rural residents to conducting fraudulent tests for toxins in the ground and water.

With a few important exceptions (Bullard 1994; Bullard and Wright 1993), discussions of "environmental justice" or "environmental victimology" have not generally considered the rural setting, except when including underdeveloped countries (e.g., Perrolle 1993; Williams 1996). This is a serious oversight because both preventing and investigating environmental crimes may be more difficult in rural areas where there may be fewer resources for identifying and responding to problems.

Another environmental crime of particular concern in rural areas is the theft of timber. This crime has been almost completely ignored by researchers, but its economic impact can be immense. In Federal forests alone, it is estimated that timber theft could total as much as $100 million each year and may account for as many as 1 in 10 trees cut in the National Forest System (Public Employees for Environmental Responsibility and the Government Accountability Project 1997; Knickerbocker 1998). Considering that only a small percentage of trees in America grow in national forests, the overall scope of tree theft may be enormous. And, as the value of wood climbs, there is also an emerging problem of the theft of particularly valuable trees. For example, large knotlike growths called burls create beautiful patterns in wood and are therefore particularly valuable. "A raw burl [from a single walnut tree] can sell for $5,000 or more in California and as much as $30,000 in Italy on the rare woods market" (Associated Press 1995). Similarly, at the time of a 1997 study, a single cedar tree could bring as much as $20,000 (Pendleton 1997).

Crimes in the name of the environment

Our interviews with rural police found that concerns about radical environmentalists were more frequently voiced in the West, where efforts to save forests in some instances have involved sabotage and in others threats to loggers and government officials. St. Clair and Cockburn (1997) have reported that the Idaho National Guard considers environmentalists among the groups posing a "hostile threat" to the State of Idaho. Throughout the country, nuclear power plants are generally located in rural areas and would be logical targets for domestic or foreign terrorists.

As the population of the United States continues to grow, sabotage and perhaps even violence will likely erupt over the use of water. Tensions over water are already high in some parts of the West, but the problem can be expected to worsen, as demand will increasingly outstrip supply.

Another likely source of environmental crime will be related to the treatment of animals in modern factory farms. Driven by small profit margins, poultry, beef, and pork producers have built large facilities into which the animals are tightly packed. Animal rights activists have increasingly focused on these large operations, in which the animals may be born and live most of their lives within a few square feet of space. The complaints of animal rights activists and of rural citizens, who object to the smell and the potential for contaminating local water supplies, are increasing in frequency. In one small Iowa town, for example, the issue of mega hog farms has divided the community, with emotions running high on both sides:

> The issue has turned meetings here of the county Board of Supervisors into such heated affairs that a panic button was installed so supervisors could summon the sheriff's office. Vandals have struck the construction sites of

some corporate hog complexes. The sheriff's department patrols them, and it tracks their sprawl with pins on its wall map. (Kilman 1995)

Ecoterrorism took yet another turn in October 1998 when an environmental group, the Earth Liberation Front, claimed credit for a fire causing more than $12 million in damage to a ski resort in Vail, Colorado. The fire was started to prevent the 885-acre expansion of a ski lodge, which the group believed would harm local wildlife (*Chicago Tribune* 1998a, 1998b). Perhaps more surprising than the act itself were the public proclamations of support for the act by spokespersons for several other activist groups.

> *An aggravated assault in a large city may become a murder in the countryside if medical help takes longer to arrive.*

America's continuous population growth means that the battles over what to do with land and natural resources will become more heated. On one hand is a growing need for the products of industries located in rural areas, such as meat processing and nuclear power, which will produce an increasing volume of hazardous waste that must be disposed of. On the other hand, as the physical size of rural America shrinks, efforts to protect what remains are likely to increase. It is from the clash of these contradictory trends that ecological crimes and civil unrest will emerge and intensify.

Contexts of Rural Crime

Recent scholarly literature on rural crime has stressed its similarity to urban crime, especially in terms of variables that predict deviant behavior (Scheer, Borden, and Donnermeyer in press) and crime rates (Rephann in press). In this chapter, however, we want to stress areas in which unique rural features may influence criminological theory, research, and criminal justice policy. We begin with a discussion of how geography and culture shape rural crime, and then argue that economic factors, demographics, and technology interact with geography and culture to shape crime in rural America.

Geography

Among the first things that come to mind when discussing rural issues are physical distance and isolation. An aggravated assault in a large city may become a murder in the countryside if medical help takes longer to arrive (cf. Doerner 1988). Similarly, the distances involved, combined with the lack of public transportation, may make it difficult for battered women to reach shelters, for victims to get to court to testify, or for offenders to attend drug treatment. Homeowners with alarm systems or the victims of violent crime may find that 911 is not available and that police response times are very slow. As one Midwestern rural sheriff told us, "They [the instructors at the State training academy] always talk about responding to a call within 2 minutes. There are parts of my county that can take an hour to get to by car." Although technology has dramatically improved the transmission of information, it has done less to speed the flow of direct human services.

Physical distance and isolation impact crime in other ways. In some rural areas, it is difficult for neighbors to watch each others' property. Plus, many rural people prefer the privacy of living in the open country with neighbors conveniently far away. Police attempting to organize neighborhood watches and other forms of community-oriented policing may find it more difficult to overcome perceptions that these activities do not apply, are not desired by rural citizens, and would be impractical to implement.

Culture

Precisely measuring and describing culture is difficult, but several features that distinguish rural from urban culture have implications for crime and justice. Among these are informal control, a mistrust of government, and a reluctance to seek outside assistance.

Informal control

There is evidence that, compared with urban areas, rural areas are more governed by informal social control. For example, Gardner and Shoemaker (1989) found that social bonding was more important in protecting against rural than urban delinquency. Smith (1980) found that in rural areas shoplifting and employee theft were rarely reported to the police. Instead, most cases were handled informally. One rural criminal justice official told Smith:

> I simply can't get people to tell me things. I hear about them two or three weeks later, and when I ask them why they didn't come to me about it, they say, "Oh, I took care of it myself." We simply can't get people to take advantage of the services of this office. (p. 52)

Informal control is facilitated by the fact that many residents of rural communities, including the local police, know each other socially:

> Everyone "knows everyone else" in small towns. Life there revolves around a core of social institutions: family, community, school, and church.

Kin, neighbors, and friends meet one another at work, at church, on Main Street, at school, or leisure activities such as high school basketball games. Daily life thus takes place among a cast of familiars whose social networks are overlapping rather than segmented. (Salamon 1997, 172)

Contributing to the familiarity of residents in many rural communities is the relative stability of the local population. Rural citizens less frequently change addresses, often staying in the same county or even the same house for several generations. Low levels of mobility and population density mean that rural police are likely to know most offenders and their families personally. If victims can identify thieves, for example, sheriffs are likely to know where to find offenders and to already know quite a bit about them.

The term "density of acquaintanceship" has been used to describe the extent to which people in a community know one another. In general, smaller communities are more likely to have a higher density of acquaintanceship. Freudenburg (1986) studied four small towns in Colorado and found that residents of communities higher in density of acquaintanceship less often reported being the victims of crime. They were also half as likely to believe it was necessary to lock their doors when they left home for a few hours or less, and they were five times less likely to believe it necessary to lock their doors when they were gone for a day or more. Similarly, high school students in high density of acquaintanceship communities were half as likely to report having felt physically threatened in their school.

Density of acquaintanceship can influence crime by increasing the watchfulness of citizens, making them more likely to feel a responsibility to act and making it easier to identify suspects. A high density of acquaintanceship can also provide for monitoring and correcting early misbehavior and delinquency. As one youth in Freudenburg's study complained, "A guy can't get away with anything around here. It seems as though, whenever I do anything wrong, my old man's found out about it before I even get home" (1986, 46).

Mistrust of government

Rural residents are more likely to be suspicious of government, particularly State and Federal governments, which are seen as insensitive to local needs. Suspicion of a strong central government is reflected in the attitudes of rural residents, who are generally less supportive than urban residents of government programs that provide welfare, housing, unemployment benefits, higher education, and Medicaid (Swanson, Cohen, and Swanson 1979). Proponents of rural development often warn against public policies dictated by a strong central government (Littrell and Littrell 1991; Seroka and Subramaniam 1991). In

1994, most police cooperated with provisions of the recently enacted Federal Brady Act, which required local police to conduct background checks on potential gun buyers. However, five rural sheriffs went to court challenging the act. Their biggest concern was the Federal Government's attempt to coerce them into enforcing the Federal law. As Sheriff J.R. Koog, of Val Verde County, Texas, remarked, "No, sir, Congress can't sit up there and tell this lowly little sheriff out here at the end of the world what to do" (Verhovek 1994, A8). Another sheriff remarked, "[T]he federal government does not have the power to conscript me to do a federal job" (Greenburg 1996, 4).

Antigovernment sentiments are particularly strong in the West, where the Federal Government controls or regulates vast areas of land and water. Government control of these resources is a sensitive issue because many residents earn their livelihood from agriculture or from such extraction industries as logging and mining. In some areas, threats of violence against Federal authorities have caused Federal agencies to stop performing some of their duties. As the *New York Times* has reported, "To wear a uniform of the Federal Government in some counties is now seen as wearing a target" (Egan 1995, A1). These threats come from a variety of individuals, even from local government officials. Mistrust of the Federal Government is also evidenced by the rise of citizen militias in the West (DeLama 1994b, 1994a). Activists in the militia movement have armed themselves in the belief that it may soon be necessary for them to use force to protect their rights. The mistrust of government expressed by militia groups has a long history in America, dating back to the origins of this country, with particularly strong ties to the countryside (Stock 1996).

Few rural citizens encourage violence against the government and fewer still directly engage in antigovernment violence. However, those expressing violent antigovernment sentiments will find more tolerance for their views among rural dwellers than urban ones.

Reluctance to seek outside assistance
Residents in rural communities tend to keep community problems to themselves, an attitude not unlike those in some urban immigrant communities. Laub (1981) found that, although the overall likelihood of reporting crime to the police was similar for rural and urban citizens, those in urban areas failed to report it because they thought nothing could be done and those in rural areas failed to report it because they considered the crime a private concern, even when the offender was a stranger.

In Weisheit's (1993, 223) study of marijuana growers, a rural police officer noted that:

> People in rural areas tend to be pretty conservative generally and don't want government coming in, or an outsider coming in, or foreigners coming in. They want the status quo and that's it. And when they develop a cancer from within they don't want it going out. They don't want people telling about it and they don't want people rocking the boat. They are the same people who will ostracize members of their society who get caught [growing marijuana].

A New Mexico State Police officer observed, "In a lot of these [rural] areas, there's really no law enforcement—no police, no sheriff, no state police station. People prefer to handle their own affairs and disputes by themselves" (Applebome 1987, 11). The officer's comment reflects two dimensions of the issue that are distinct but reinforce each other. First, rural citizens may less often choose to deal with a problem formally because they see it as a personal problem. Second, in some rural areas, formal police authority is in fact physically distant and is not an immediate option.

Economic factors

Economic conditions in rural America vary widely, from growth and prosperity to decline and abject poverty. Many rural areas adjacent to large metropolitan areas have experienced rapid growth in population and economic activity (Johnson and Beale 1995). Other rural communities are realizing economic benefits from modern technology and from the siting of manufacturing in their communities. Advances in technology have meant that some kinds of work can be done anywhere the worker has access to telephone lines. As Hackenberg and Kukulka (1995, 190) note:

> Small Midwestern towns, where property values have fallen for decades, are linked to the financial and population centers on the Atlantic, Pacific, and Gulf coasts by communications technology. Creative work, clerical operations, billing and marketing, sales promotions, and consulting services can all be economically provided from these accessible points on the information highway.

Fairfield, Iowa, for example, is a community of approximately 10,000 people, nearly 60 miles from the nearest interstate highway. It is also home to Telegroup, Inc., and Global Link, both of which sell long distance international telephone services and have annual sales exceeding $300 million (Van 1997).

A number of rural communities have benefited from the location of modern manufacturing plants. Inexpensive property, cheap labor, low crime, lax zoning, and low taxes make many rural areas appealing to industries of all kinds.

> *The lengths to which some rural communities go to attract prisons is a testament to the current economic condition of these areas and the perceived prospects for other forms of economic development.*

Some bring long-term prosperity, while others exploit rural communities by moving whenever the next town offers a better deal. The most obvious example of how manufacturing has impacted rural communities is the tendency for new automobile assembly plants to site in rural locations (Gelsanliter 1990). These plants bring economic and population growth, but local communities may also experience an increase in crime and social disruption. For example, in Spring Hill, Tennessee, a Saturn automobile plant opened in the late 1980s, doubling the population to 1,464 people. Commercial growth followed, as did crime: "'Worst crime before Saturn arrived?' said Paul Williams, a former police chief. 'I don't know. Weekend drunks, maybe.' Now, the police force, which has grown to seven, from four, has to deal with more serious problems, like drugs" (Janofsky 1993, 20).

One police chief with whom we spoke anticipated that the opening of a large Federal building in his area would result in an increase in burglary because "now that people will have jobs, they will also have VCRs and other things worth stealing. Until now there hasn't been much for a would-be burglar to take."

In contrast to the prosperity of rural communities adjacent to urban areas, many remote rural communities have not experienced growth and have long suffered from poverty, unemployment, and underemployment. For the economically disadvantaged "backwaters" of rural America, there is little reason to believe that circumstances will improve in the near future. As Lyson and Falk (1993, 3–4) note in their focus on nine economically lagging regions of the United States:

> Today, lagging rural regions are best viewed within a larger global economy. The socioeconomic gap between rural America and urban America has begun to widen. . . . The occupational structure is fragmenting into well-paying jobs for highly skilled, well-educated, technologically sophisticated workers and low-paying, low-skill, service jobs. Migration no longer offers the same opportunity for people in forgotten places to improve their economic lot as it did even a generation ago (Wilson, 1987). Within lagging rural regions, branch plants are closing their doors and moving to Third World locations where wages are even lower and workers

less organized than in the economic backwaters of the United States (Lyson, 1989). The forgotten places . . . are being by-passed in the newly forming global economy.

One sign of desperate economic circumstances is the effort by many rural communities to attract prisons:

> A generation ago, rural America found the notion of accepting a prison so repellent that many communities sued their state governments to keep them out. . . . [today] small towns from California to Florida are battling to get a penitentiary in their backyard. In many cases they are offering free land, utilities and cash incentives for the chance to get a slice of what is turning out to be the public works mega-project of the 1990s. In jobs and job security, prisons are doing for Main Street U.S.A. what military bases did during the cold war. (Lamb 1996)

The percentage of prison inmates housed in nonmetropolitan counties has increased steadily over time (Beale 1993). In general, prisons are attractive to the same economically depressed areas that are willing to house other undesirable industries, including power plants, new landfills, hazardous waste facilities, and recovery plants for garbage (Shichor 1992). For builders, these areas have the advantages of high unemployment, low labor costs, little or no union representation, and lax or nonexistent zoning regulations.

The long-term impact of prison construction on economic development and crime is unclear. A prison may provide stable employment, but the stigma of having prisons may make it more difficult to attract other businesses (Moberg 1996). At best, prisons halt or slow economic decay, saving communities from economic ruin, but also preventing dramatic growth. The lengths to which some rural communities go to attract prisons is a testament to the current economic condition of these areas and the perceived prospects for other forms of economic development.

There is no clear evidence that the threat to citizens from prison escapes is a serious problem, nor is there conclusive evidence that a prison brings an increase in local crime (Shichor 1992). Prison visitors do not generally move to the area, nor do inmates generally settle in the area upon their release, but both patterns may change. We know of at least one rural community in which gang leaders who run drug operations from their prison cells have had confederates move to the community to facilitate communication with outside operatives. Research in Oregon found that released inmates often remained in the local community for aftercare programs, which were required as a condition of parole

The U.S. Immigration and Naturalization Service estimates that as many as 25 percent of the meat processing workers in the Midwest are illegal aliens. Taking such economically dispossessed immigrants and putting them into culturally homogeneous small communities creates the potential for racial tensions and hate crimes.

(Caillier and Versteeg 1988). As the drive to build more prisons continues, and as new prisons are sited in rural areas, it will become crucial to understand why crime increases follow the arrival of prisons in some communities and not others.

Efforts to spur economic growth in rural areas have sometimes increased crime-related problems while having little impact on the economic vitality of the area. Particularly questionable is the pursuit of rural economic development by promoting tourism and recruiting low-skill, labor-intensive industries, such as meat and poultry processing plants. Local policy-makers often assume that increased employment betters the lives of residents, but wages and benefits in some industries are so low that full-time employees still have incomes well below the poverty level. Reduced unemployment thus may only shift people from unemployed poor to working poor (Browne et al. 1992).

Gouveia and Stull (1995) illustrate this problem in their examination of the impact of two large meat-packing plants near the small community of Garden City, Kansas. Because of technological advances in meat processing, these new jobs were all unskilled. Consequently, wages in these plants were low, and wages in the newly created service sector were even lower. As a result, per capita county income dropped from 94 percent of the State average in 1980 to 91.5 percent of the State average in 1988—more than $1,300 below the State average and $2,111 below the national average (Gouveia and Stull 1995). In addition to being low paying, the work was demanding and injuries were frequent; as many as 4 in 10 meat processing workers were injured each year (Stull and Broadway 1995). Because the local population was not large enough to meet the labor needs of the plants, workers were recruited from across the country. Mobile home parks sprang up to house the workers, and social problems soon followed. School enrollment soared, particularly for minority and bilingual students. "In 1990, Garden City's school district had the highest dropout rate in Kansas, student turnover of almost one-third each year, and chronic absenteeism" (Gouveia and Stull 1995, 91). Demands on temporary shelters increased 2.5 times in just 6 years, and crime increased dramatically. "Both violent and property crime climbed throughout the decade in Finney County, while falling in the state. The incidence of child abuse more than tripled to exceed the state average by 50 percent" (Gouveia and Stull 1995, 91). Such areas are also likely to have an inadequate tax base to fully support the increased demands placed on the criminal justice system, a problem compounded by the common practice of extending generous tax incentives initially to attract processing plants.

Some of the largest operations are sited in communities of only 1,100 or 1,200 people, far beyond the capacity of local residents to supply the required labor needs (Hackenberg 1995). Consequently, companies recruit unskilled immigrants, particularly Asians and Hispanics, who are desperate for work. There are allegations that the companies also recruit directly in Mexico. The U.S. Immigration and Naturalization Service estimates that as many as 25 percent of the meat processing workers in the Midwest are illegal aliens (Heges, Hawkins, and Loeb 1996). Taking such economically dispossessed immigrants and putting them into culturally homogeneous small communities creates the potential for racial tensions and hate crimes. It is also unlikely that the justice systems in these rural communities are prepared to handle culturally diverse populations. Solving the problems described in the meat and poultry processing industries is complicated by the rise of a world economy in which cheap labor in underdeveloped countries competes directly with cheap labor in the United States.

The potential long-term impact of these low-wage, labor-intensive industries is disturbing. Rural Americans have a long history of mistrust and even hostility toward the government and the banking industry (Stock 1996). Dyer (1997) argues that the farm crisis of the 1980s revived and fueled existing antigovernment and antibanking sentiments throughout rural America. Feeling victimized and powerless in the legitimate political and economic system, many became sympathetic to the arguments of militias and other antigovernment groups. Similar reactions seem likely to the continued use of rural areas to site industries that are dangerous for employees while providing neither a living wage nor adequate fringe benefits.

Demographic factors

For much of its history, the United States has been a predominantly rural society. In 1790, for example, there were only 8 communities in the United States with more than 5,000 people, and the entire population of the United States was less than 4 million people. In 1917, a majority of the United States' population, for the first time, was urban. Today nearly three-fourths of the population of the United States lives in urban areas. It is not that rural areas have lost population; they simply have not grown as fast as urban areas.

Historically, as the United States' population has shifted from rural to urban areas, young skilled workers moved from the countryside to the city, economically dispossessed minorities moved to cities seeking employment opportunities, and foreign immigrants settled mainly in the largest cities. The rural population continued to grow because rural families were large, offsetting the effects of outmigration. In the 1970s, these patterns changed. The "rural turnaround" began. Rural areas started growing because urban residents were moving into the countryside in larger numbers. Many were seeking the amenities commonly associated with rural areas, both from the physical environment (e.g., mountains, lakes) and from a social environment in which crime and other urban ills were less pronounced. Although economic conditions in the 1980s slowed the flow of people into the countryside, the strong economy of the 1990s once again saw many rural areas gain population as a result of net inmigration. Those moving from the city were often retirees, commuters, or adults drawn to recreation (Edmondson 1997; Johnson and Beale 1995). Among rural areas, the greatest growth has been in communities within commuting distance of metropolitan areas, in retirement communities, and in communities that have attracted manufacturing or service industries. While economically vital rural areas experience population increases, economically depressed rural areas continue to lose citizens over time as young people move out and those who stay age in place (Johnson and Beale 1995).

The number of people age 65 years and older in the United States is increasing at a 2.4-percent annual rate. "By the year 2025 at the latest, the proportion of all Americans who are elderly will be the same as the proportion in Florida today. America, in effect, will become a nation of Floridas—and then keep aging. By 2040, one in four Americans may be over sixty-five" (Peterson 1996, 15). Contributing to the aging of rural America is a decline in rural family size over the past 50 years. Population growth fueled by adult inmigration rather than births means that the rural population is aging even more rapidly than is urban America.

The graying of America's population will have an impact on rural America. Drawn by a lower cost of living, relatively less crime, and a slower pace, small towns and rural areas have been popular retirement locations. As the number of retirees continues to grow, the number who retire to rural areas will also grow. The full implications of this demographic shift on crime are unclear, but several outcomes seem likely. First, because the crime rate among senior citizens is very low, and many senior citizens have relatively good financial resources, the number of crimes committed by these citizens should be substantially fewer than those committed by a comparable number of young people. In particular, violent crimes should be less frequent. Second, crimes *against* the elderly will probably increase, including health insurance fraud, fraud in home repairs, and elder abuse by care providers and family members. Third, some forms of crimes *by* the elderly will likely increase, including Medicare fraud and the illegal sale of prescription medicines. Fourth, fear of crime is high among seniors. The large number of senior citizens and their propensity to vote may make rural crime control an increasingly important legislative agenda item.

Continued population growth and urban sprawl will mean a steady reduction in the number of rural areas and a continuous supply of places in transition from rural to suburban or urban. "Across the nation, 1 million acres of farmland are being converted to urban or suburban uses each year, a rate of two acres per minute" (Brandon 1996). In California's Central Valley, for example, it is estimated that, by the year 2040, the population will triple and housing will consume more than 1 million acres of irrigated farmland (Goldberg 1996).

Rapidly growing rural communities may see crime increase three to four times faster than the population (Freudenburg and Jones 1991). These areas also are subject to "spillover crime" from urban centers, such as increased gang activity (Wells and Weisheit 1998). Some States have reported an increase in the phenomenon of urban bank robbers going to outlying areas, where they believe the banks will be easier targets. Police have even revived a century-old word to describe these robbers—"yeggs" (*Law Enforcement News* 1997). Growth is likely to put a financial strain on criminal justice resources and to foster divisiveness in rural communities (Johnson and Beale 1995).

Technological factors

America's shift from being predominantly rural to predominantly urban has been largely due to developments in technology. As fertile farmland is taken out of production, farmers will be increasingly pressured to maximize yields on the land that remains. This will mean an even greater reliance on pesticides, herbicides, and concentrated fertilizers. The theft of farm chemicals is already a problem and is likely to become more serious (e.g., Johnson 1994). Because they are sold in highly concentrated forms and difficult to tag with identifying markers, the theft of farm chemicals may become simpler and more lucrative than the theft of livestock or farm machinery. A 1992 report from California indicated that pesticide thefts were becoming more frequent and more expensive, with the typical replacement value of a single theft between $30,000 and $70,000 (Pesticide Action Network North America Update Service 1992). More recently, California officials brought charges against a man for fencing $1.5 million worth of stolen herbicides (*Evansville [Indiana] Courier* 1995). Commonly used varieties can sell for $175 for a 5-gallon case. The most concentrated and expensive herbicides can sell for as much as $115 for only 7.5 ounces, which will cover nearly 5 acres. It is possible to carry more than

$500,000 of this concentrated herbicide in the back of a pickup truck (Smith 1996). Given these prices, the profits for thieves can be substantial, with correspondingly large losses for farmers. Despite the magnitude of losses, little is known about the structure of these theft operations.

One countertrend to the increased use of chemicals is found in new agricultural practices, such as no-till and organic farming. However, these practices require more expensive farm machinery. Farming has come to rely heavily on machine technology. The modern mega hog farm, for example, relies so much on technology that the average hog requires only about 12 minutes of human attention during the 4 months it takes to grow to maturity (Kilman 1995). Mechanization requires a greater capital investment, making farms more attractive targets for theft and vandalism.

The costs of raising livestock also add to the problem. Artificial insemination is the commonly accepted way to impregnate dairy and beef cattle. The semen of prize bulls can be worth thousands of dollars at an auction. The editor of a farm journal in an Eastern State described to us how thieves removed from a ranch two $80,000 nitrogen tanks that stored frozen bull semen.

As farms and ranches become larger, requiring more machinery and other expensive agricultural technologies, and as many more are operated by corporations rather than families, employee theft will become a greater problem. For example, one investigator in Florida noted that many cattle thefts are committed by present or former employees. These individuals often work long hours for low wages, are transient or provide seasonal labor, and have little financial or emotional investment in the farm or the farm owner. They make arrangements with auction houses and slaughterhouses to fence stolen animals for cash. For both farm machinery and livestock thefts, technology facilitates the commission of crimes. Large trucks to haul stolen goods and a highway system that makes many rural areas easily accessible mean that physical isolation no longer provides the same level of protection against theft. The Attorney General's Office for the State of Iowa, for example, found that most agricultural crimes occurred within about 20 miles of either side of the interstate highways that run through the State (Statistical Analysis Center 1985).

The rise of factories, which required workers to gather in a single location, made cities the centers of economic development. Initially, this rural-to-urban movement resulted in a net loss of people from rural areas. However, in recent decades, a reverse migration pattern has occurred as industries, businesses, and people have moved out of metropolitan centers to surrounding areas. Demographers have described this latter pattern as *deconcentration*, reflecting "a long-term and gradual dispersal of the United States' population into smaller, less densely settled cities and towns" (Johnson and Beale 1995). Deconcentration is driven by technological changes that allow more work to take place in less urban locations, as dominant industries change from large-scale manufacturing (which requires large urban centers to be efficient) to information management, knowledge creation, and service provision (which does not).

However, technological advances have not benefited all rural residents. A 1997 report by the California Institute for Rural Studies argued that advances in technology, combined with changes in the use of migrant labor, resulted in real wages that were lower than they were 20 years earlier (Schodolski 1997). Thus, for some rural Americans, technology has served to hasten the decline in living standards.

The impact of technology will probably be very different for the wealthiest and for the poorest rural citizens. Technology will work *for* those citizens who are better educated and who already have a higher standard of living. It will facilitate telecommuting, distance learning, and the development of small businesses that utilize communications networks to provide services, such as technical assistance, or to ship information-based products, such as computer software. Technology is likely to work *against* the poorest rural citizens whose livelihoods are based on labor-intensive jobs. The skills required for these jobs will decline as technology advances, and wages will decline as rural workers increasingly compete with unskilled workers in underdeveloped countries.

Technological advances will not be equally available to all rural areas. The wealthiest rural areas and those near large metropolitan areas likely will be among the first to have access to modern technological advances. By contrast, the poorest rural areas likely will be among the last to benefit from technology. Consider, for example, that households outside metropolitan areas are about twice as likely as those inside metropolitan areas to be without telephones. Perhaps the most dramatic illustration is in rural Kentucky, where one in five nonmetropolitan counties has more than 20 percent of homes without telephone service (U.S. Bureau of the Census 1993). Although urban residents without phones can often find one next door or down the block, in rural areas, the nearest phone may be a considerable distance away, and some rural areas still are not served by cellular telephone service providers.

Technology's impact on rural America has been substantial, but the impact of future technological developments on rural crime is not clear. Such predictions require the ability to anticipate new technologies, as well as the ability to imagine how those technologies might be turned to criminal advantage. Both have proven difficult to anticipate, but we can make informed speculation. The advent of satellite communications, electronic banking, shared computer databases of personal information, and the Internet will generate new kinds of crimes. These new crimes will involve electronic access to information, or digital codes, that depend on electronic connectivity and communication access that is almost unrelated to physical distance. It will make rural citizens as vulnerable as urban residents to the new forms of crime, including electronic fraud, theft, vandalism, trespassing, even personal abuse such as harassment, threats, and cyberstalking (Banks 1997).

Race, Ethnicity, and Crime in Rural America

The link between race, ethnicity, and crime in rural areas is understudied. In general, rural areas are more racially homogenous than large cities. In central cities, whites comprise about 66 percent of the population, but in rural areas, they account for more than 90 percent of the population (see exhibit 6). In some large industrial States with diverse urban populations, such as Illinois, Michigan, and New York, the rural population is more than 97 percent white. In seven States, minorities are better represented in rural than urban areas: Alaska, Arizona, Idaho, Montana, New Mexico, North Dakota, and South Dakota. In these States, there are large Native American (or Eskimo) and/or Mexican-American populations. As exhibit 6 shows, Native Americans are among the only minority groups in America better represented in rural areas than in central cities (U.S. Bureau of the Census 1990).

Exhibit 6. Percentage of the population in selected race or ethnic categories in central cities and rural areas*

Race/ethnic category	Percentage in central cities	Percentage in rural areas
White	66.2	90.6
Black	22.0	6.2
American Indian	0.6	1.3
Asian	4.2	0.5
Hispanic	14.8	3.1

* Column percentages do not total 100 because some categories of race are not included and because the Census Bureau treats "Hispanic" as an ethnicity and not a race, allowing for overlap between categories of race and ethnicity.

Source: U.S. Bureau of the Census 1990, table 3.

These national averages do not reveal the complete picture. First, most of the racial-ethnic differential between rural and urban areas is due to differences in the proportion of minorities in central cities. Second, rural areas differ greatly in the composition of their population, reflecting large regional variations. For example, with only three exceptions, all nonmetropolitan counties with a black population exceeding 20 percent are located in the South. Nonmetropolitan counties with a Mexican-American population that is greater than 20 percent are located exclusively in the Southwest. Nonmetropolitan counties with substantial Native American populations are mostly west of the Mississippi River.

It appears that the link between race and crime differs somewhat across rural, suburban, and urban areas. Bachman's (1992a) examination of NCVS data revealed that, in urban areas, blacks had higher victimization rates than whites for violent crimes. In rural areas, the violent crime victimization rate for whites was higher. For property crimes such as burglary and household larceny, blacks had higher rates of victimization across community sizes.

Using NCVS data, Laub (1983) estimated personal crime offense rates for communities of varying sizes. He found that race differences across community sizes varied by age. For example, black/white differences in offense rates for juveniles were greater in central cities than outside central cities. For adults, these differences (by community size) practically disappeared.

Although urban studies of the street-level drug trade reflect a high representation of minorities, Weisheit's (1992) study of rural marijuana cultivators found no involvement by blacks and only a few cases of involvement by Hispanics. Anecdotal evidence also suggests the lack of involvement of minorities in rural methamphetamine laboratories.

A related issue is the way minorities are handled in the criminal justice system. Most studies have found that minorities are overrepresented in the justice system. However, nearly all such studies are conducted in urban areas. One study of juvenile offenders in the State of Washington found substantial variations across counties (Bridges 1993). Areas where minorities were overrepresented had three features in common: (1) most of their population lived in cities, (2) there was a large minority population, and (3) the violent crime rate was high. While this was the general pattern, not every metropolitan county showed high disproportionality and not every rural county showed low disproportionality. Interpreting these findings is complicated by the small minority populations in many rural counties. For example, in 1990, 23 of Washington's 34 counties had small minority populations and sentenced no minority youths to confinement.

Although crime among American Indians has been given some attention (e.g., Mann 1993; Nielsen and Silverman 1996), little research focuses on comparing rural and urban patterns of crime or variations in crime across rural Native American groups. Crime among American Indians in rural areas is in particular need of further study. There are great differences in the histories and cultures of American Indian groups. Geography and economic factors add to the complexity, combined with a dizzying array of jurisdictional issues and criminal justice structures (cf. Baker 1993; Canby 1988; Deloria and Lytle 1983; Green and Tonnesen 1991).

American Indians appear to have high rates of child abuse and very high rates of alcohol-related offenses compared with other groups. Obtaining accurate crime figures is always difficult, but may be particularly so in Indian Country, where tribal police may be seriously underfunded (depending on the tribe), may have few incentives for officially reporting crime to the FBI, and may operate in cultures that are often closed to outsiders, even by rural standards.

At least two studies focus on American Indian crime and include rural-urban comparisons. Jensen, Stauss, and Harris (1977), using several data sources, found that crime rates for American Indians were higher than for whites, blacks, or Asian-Americans. They also found that white/Native American differences were smaller in rural areas than in urban areas. Native American crime rates in urban areas were four times those of whites, while in rural areas the crime rate was only about 2.5 times higher.

More recently, Greenfeld and Smith (1999) assembled information about American Indian crime using both victimization data and official police data from UCR. Self-reported victimization data showed substantial variations across rural, suburban, and urban areas and between American Indians and other racial groups. Exhibit 7 shows that violent victimization was higher among American Indians than any other racial group. In fact, rural American Indians had higher victimization rates than urban blacks. And, except for Asians, victimization rates for each racial group were lowest in rural areas.

The future crime problems of Native Americans will depend heavily on the social and economic circumstances of these groups. Recent changes in the economic circumstances of some Native American groups following the legalization of gambling indicate the need for caution about assuming that future economic and crime patterns are likely to be simple extensions of current patterns.

Exhibit 7. Violent victimization by race

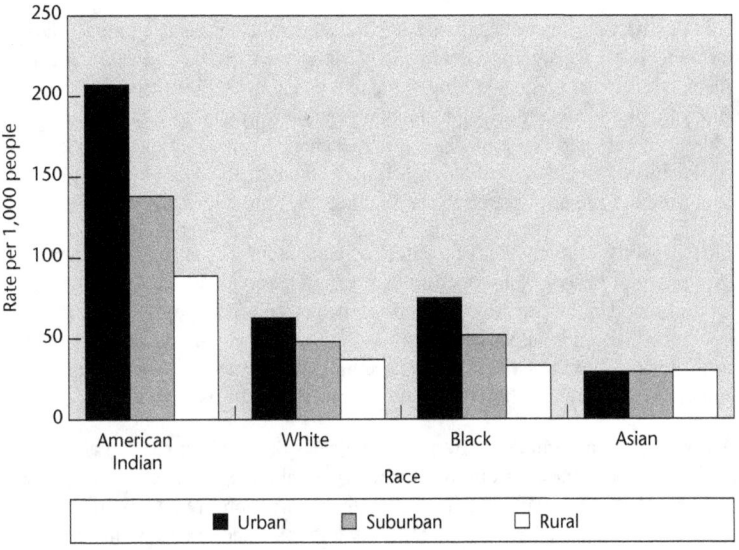

Source: Created from data presented in Greenfeld and Smith 1999.

Although research about crime among rural American Indians is relatively sparse, it appears full and rich compared with studies of other rural minority groups. For example, very little is known about rural-urban differences in crime among Hispanic and Asian populations. Self-report studies of delinquency, especially substance use, indicate lower rates among rural Hispanics than among rural whites and blacks. However, Hispanic dropout rates are much higher. One study indicated that Mexican-American adolescents who drop out of high school are more likely than white dropouts to be involved in violence, as both perpetrators and victims (Chavez, Oetting, and Swaim 1994).

So little is known about crime among rural Asian-Americans that predictions about future patterns in this group are impossible. Anecdotal evidence indicates that some groups have been subjected to hate crimes. For example, one group of Vietnamese living in a coastal area of one Southern State was the target of vandalism and harassment as it took up its traditional occupation of fishing, in direct competition with local fishermen.

What Does the Future Hold?

Rural crime, as with crime in general, is the result of a confluence of many factors. Technology, geography, demography, economics, and culture all interact to shape rural crime. Predicting rural crime requires accurately anticipating how each of these factors will change and how relationships among them will change. Moreover, the rapid development of a global economy and improvements in communications and transportation will likely increase the speed at which international developments are felt in rural settings.

This all points to many areas for future research. Our discussion has focused on the variety of factors that shape rural crime and on contemporary rural crime issues in the United States. Other issues, such as considerations of rural crime over time, international variations in rural crime, and variations in crime among rural areas within the United States have had to be neglected. Comparing rural and urban crime, as we have done throughout this essay, is only a first step.

A careful look at rural crime over time indicates the need for caution about regarding future variations in rural crime as simple linear projections from the present. Although homicide today generally occurs more frequently in urban areas than rural areas, this was not always true (cf. Lane 1997). As historians Johnson and Monkkonen (1996, 1) observed in their analysis of crime in Europe since the Middle Ages:

> Over time there have been both large and subtle shifts in this elemental dichotomy [between violent crime in cities and in the countryside]. The classic city had walls to keep armies and criminals out. Gangs were in the countryside. Today, at least in the suburbs and rural parts of the United States, many people would like to wall cities to keep criminals and gangs in.

Thus, the relatively low violent crime rate now typical of rural areas should be viewed as a variable that merits explanation.

In addition to studying variations over time, future research will benefit from an analysis of variations in rural crime across cultures. Although there has been some rural crime research in other countries, particularly in Australia (Jobes et al. 1999), rural crime in non-Western societies has been studied infrequently. Much of the work that has been done on crime in non-Western societies has been carried out by anthropologists, whose work generally has not been used by criminologists to advance criminological theory (Moss 1997). And, the nature of the discipline discourages the development of broad theories of crime by anthropologists themselves.

More needs to be done to examine variations in crime among rural areas in the United States. Provocative work focusing primarily on regional variations in rural American violence has been conducted by Nisbett and Cohen (1996), who observed that high homicide rates in the South are almost entirely the result of very high rates among white rural males. For females and for minority males, there are only minor differences between homicide rates in the South and in other regions of the country. Nisbett and Cohen argue that these high rates are the result of a "culture of honor," in which violence is an accepted response to an affront to one's home, family, or person. They build a persuasive argument that the culture of honor can be traced to the type of agricultural activity in which the region's ancestors engaged. Nisbett and Cohen and others (e.g., Fischer 1989) make a powerful case for incorporating community size, regional history, race, and gender into analyses of violence in America. Their work is a good example of the utility of incorporating variations among rural areas in explanations of crime.

The work of Sampson and associates (Sampson 1986; Sampson and Groves 1989; Sampson, Raudenbush, and Earls 1997) on the relationship between crime and the economic and social characteristics of urban communities should be extended to the study of rural communities. Because 88 percent of the incorporated communities in America have less than 10,000 people (Hobbs 1994), and because many of these small communities are rural and relatively self-contained, they offer the advantage of numbers of communities and variability, allowing for rigorous statistical testing of structural theories of crime, such as the social disorganization theory. Many, but not all, rural places have relatively less "contaminating" interaction with adjacent areas than occurs in most urban places, and this contamination is itself a variable worth including in studies of crime.

Sampson and Castellano's 1982 analysis of the relationship between economic inequality and crime provides an excellent example of how including rural communities can help clarify and specify theories of crime and point to new directions for research. They found that economic inequality and criminal victimization were inversely related in urban areas, but not in rural areas, and they provided a thoughtful discussion of the implications for theories based on economic inequality.

This chapter has illustrated some of the many factors that shape rural crime. It has also used examples to argue that understanding rural crime requires understanding rural life. The study of rural crime provides a continuous reminder that a thorough understanding of crime requires a thorough understanding of the contexts in which crimes occur. Although some recent theories of crime have emphasized daily life and routine activities, these formulations have generally ignored the rural setting and have consequently missed the contributions that might come from including a rural perspective (Weisheit and Wells 1996). By juxtaposing our understanding of the environments in which rural and urban crime occur, it may be possible to improve our general understanding of crime.

This chapter has focused on factors that will shape the future of rural crime, but those same factors will shape the administration of justice in rural America (Weisheit and Kernes 1997; Weisheit, Wells, and Falcone 1994). The overlapping social networks and high density of acquaintanceship that influence both the criminal offender and the victim also influence agents of the justice system. Rural police, judges, and probation officers are much more likely than their urban counterparts to live in the communities in which they work. Citizens recognize them and consider them on duty even when they are not wearing their uniforms. Many of them grew up in the same communities in which they work and must handle cases involving friends and relatives. Rural judges and prosecutors sometimes must proceed against members of their own families, something that would be unthinkable in most cities. In urban areas, criminal justice officials are able to make a distinction between their public and private lives that is far more difficult to draw in rural communities. Many crimes are problems in both urban and rural areas, but the contexts in which they occur and in which they are responded to are very different. Perhaps this is why rural police are able to clear a substantially higher percentage of known offenses than urban police. Perhaps this is why rural residents are less likely to believe police brutality is a problem in their communities. It is probably true everywhere that the same contextual factors that shape crime shape the community's response to it. In rural areas, however, it is impossible to ignore the connection.

References

Angell, Ian. 1992. Winners and losers in the information age. *Society* 34:81–85.

Angle, Paul. 1980. *Bloody Williamson*. New York: Alfred A. Knopf.

Applebome, Peter. 1987. Some say frontier is still there, and still different. *New York Times* 12 December.

Arthur, John A. 1991. Socioeconomic predictors of crime in rural Georgia. *Criminal Justice Review* 16:29–41.

Associated Press. 1995. Thieves destroying walnut trees for valuable wood. 9 October. Retrieved 16 January 1997 from the World Wide Web: http://sddt.com/files/librarywire/DN95_10_09/DN95_10_09_1.htm.

Bachman, Ronet. 1992a. *Crime victimization in city, suburban, and rural areas*. Report, NCJ 135943. Washington, D.C.: U.S. Department of Justice. Bureau of Justice Statistics.

————. 1992b. Crime in nonmetropolitan America: A national accounting of trends, incidence rates, and idiosyncratic vulnerabilities. *Rural Sociology* 57:546–560.

Badger, Lee W. 1989. Reporting of child abuse: Influence of characteristics of physician, practice, and community. *Southern Medical Journal* 82:281–286.

Bai, Matt. 1997. White storm warning: In Fargo and the Prairie States, speed kills. *Newsweek*, 31 March, 66.

Baker, B.T. 1993. *Law enforcement within Indian nations*. Glynco, Georgia: Federal Law Enforcement Training Center.

Baker, James N., Patricia King, Andrew Murr, and Nonny Abbott. 1989. The newest drug war: In rural America, crack and "crank" are now hot commodities in the backwoods. *Newsweek*, 3 April, 20–22.

Banks, Michael A. 1997. *Web psychos, stalkers, and pranksters*. Albany: Coriolis Group.

Bankston, William B., and David H. Allen. 1980. Rural social areas and patterns of homicide: An analysis of lethal violence in Louisiana. *Rural Sociology* 45:223–237.

Bastian, Lisa D. 1995. *Criminal victimization 1993*. Report, NCJ 151658. Washington, D.C.: U.S. Department of Justice, Bureau of Justice Statistics.

Bastian, Lisa D., and Taylor, Bruce M. 1991. *School crime: A National Crime Victimization Survey report*. NCJ 131641. Washington, D.C.: U.S. Department of Justice, Bureau of Justice Statistics.

Beale, C. 1993. Prisons, population, and jobs in nonmetro America. *Rural Development Perspectives* 8:16–19.

Belyea, Michael J., and Matthew T. Zingraff. 1985. Monitoring rural-urban drug trends: An analysis of drug arrest statistics, 1976–1980. *International Journal of the Addictions* 20:369–380.

Brandon, Karen. 1996. Suburbia sprouts in California's valley of plenty. *Chicago Tribune*, 18 November.

Bridges, George S. 1993. Racial disproportionality in the juvenile justice system. Report submitted to the Commission on African American Affairs and Management Services Division/Department of Social and Health Services, State of Washington, Olympia, Washington.

Brodsky, Harold. 1990. Emergency medical service rescue time in fatal road accidents. *Transportation Research Record* 1270:89–96.

Browne, William P., Jerry R. Skees, Louis E. Swanson, Paul B. Thompson, and Laurian J. Unnevehr. 1992. *Sacred cows and hot potatoes: Agrarian myths in agricultural policy*. Boulder, Colorado: Westview Press.

Bullard, Robert D. 1994. *Unequal protection: Environmental justice & communities of color*. San Francisco: Sierra Club Books.

Bullard, Robert D., and Beverly Wright. 1993. *Confronting environmental racism: Voices from the grassroots*. Somerville, Massachusetts: South End Press.

Caillier, Mark W., and Karyn D. Versteeg. 1988. *Preliminary conclusions: Correctional impact on the city of Salem police services*. Salem, Oregon: Salem Police Department. Cited in David Shichor, Myths and realities in prison siting, *Crime & Delinquency* 38 (1992): 70–87.

Canby, William C., Jr. 1988. *American Indian law*. 2d ed. St. Paul: West Publishing Company.

Castellano, Thomas C., and Craig D. Uchida. 1990. Local drug enforcement, prosecutors, and case attrition: Theoretical perspectives for the drug war. *American Journal of Police* 9:133–162.

Chavez, Ernie L., Gene R. Oetting, and Randy C. Swaim. 1994. Dropout and delinquency: Mexican-American and Caucasian non-Hispanic youth. *Journal of Clinical Child Psychology* 23:47–55.

Chicago Tribune. 1998a. Group claims it set fires at ski resort to preserve lynx. 22 October.

———. 1998b. Vail attack called sign of growing eco-terrorism. 23 October.

———. 1997. Vandals free thousands of minks. 2 June.

———. 1989. Illegal drug trade spreads to rural areas. 4 August.

Clayton, Richard R. 1995. *Marijuana in the "Third World": Appalachia, U.S.A.* Boulder, Colorado: Lynne Reinner Publishers.

Cronk, Christine, and Paul D. Sarvela. 1997. Alcohol, tobacco, and other drug use among rural and urban youth: A secondary analysis of the Monitoring the Future data set. *American Journal of Public Health* 87:760–764.

DeLama, George. 1994a. For militias, invaders of U.S. are everywhere. *Chicago Tribune*, 31 October.

———. 1994b. West chomping at the bit over Federal control. *Chicago Tribune*, 27 October.

Deloria, Vine, Jr., and Clifford M. Lytle. 1983. *American Indians, American justice*. Austin: University of Texas Press.

Doerner, William G. 1988. The impact of medical resources on criminally induced lethality: A further examination. *Criminology* 26:171–179.

Donnermeyer, Joseph F. 1994. Crime and violence in rural communities. Paper presented at the 1994 Annual Meeting of the Academy of Criminal Justice Sciences, Chicago.

————. 1992. The use of alcohol, marijuana, and hard drugs by rural adolescents: A review of recent research. In *Drug use in rural American communities*, edited by Ruth W. Edwards. New York: Haworth Press.

Donnermeyer, Joseph F., and G. Howard Phillips. 1982. The nature of vandalism among rural youth. In *Rural crime: Integrating research and prevention*, edited by Timothy J. Carter, G. Howard Phillips, Joseph F. Donnermeyer, and Todd N. Wurschmidt. Totowa, New Jersey: Allanheld, Osmun.

Dyer, Joel. 1997. *Harvest of rage: Why Oklahoma City is only the beginning*. Boulder, Colorado: Westview Press.

Edmondson, B. 1997. A new era for rural America. *American Demographics* 17:30–31.

Egan, Timothy. 1995. Federal uniforms become target of wave of threats and violence. *New York Times*, 25 April.

Evansville (Indiana) Courier. 1995. Farm thieves reaping big profits from agricultural chemicals. 30 April.

Fischer, Claude S. 1980. The spread of violent crime from city to countryside, 1955 to 1975. *Rural Sociology* 45:416–434.

Fischer, David Hackett. 1989. *Albion's seed: Four British folkways in America*. New York: Oxford University Press.

Flynn, Kevin, and Gary Gerhardt. 1989. *The silent brotherhood: Inside America's racist underground*. New York: Free Press.

Freudenburg, William R. 1986. The density of acquaintanceship: An overlooked variable in community research. *American Journal of Sociology* 92:27–63.

Freudenburg, William R., and Robert Emmett Jones. 1991. Criminal behavior and rapid community growth: Examining the evidence. *Rural Sociology* 56:619–645.

Frisch, S. 1997. Mink farmers brace for vandalism wave. *Chicago Tribune*, 13 November.

Gagne, Patricia L. 1992. Appalachian women: Violence and social control. *Journal of Contemporary Ethnography* 20:387–415.

Gardner, LeGrande, and Donald J. Shoemaker. 1989. Social bonding and delinquency: A comparative analysis. *The Sociological Quarterly* 30:481–500.

Gelsanliter, David. 1990. *Jump start: Japan comes to the heartland*. New York: Farrar, Straus & Giroux.

Goldberg, Carey. 1996. Alarm bells sounding as suburbs gobble up California's richest farmland. *New York Times*, 20 June.

Gouveia, Lourdes, and Donald D. Stull. 1995. Dances with cows: Beefpacking's impact on Garden City, Kansas, and Lexington, Nebraska. In *Any way you cut it: Meat processing and small-town America*, edited Donald D. Stull, Michael J. Broadway, and David Griffith. Lawrence: University Press of Kansas.

Green, Donald E., and Thomas V. Tonnesen, eds. 1991. *American Indians: Social justice and public policy*. Milwaukee: University of Wisconsin System, Institute on Race and Ethnicity.

Greenburg, Jan Crawford. 1996. Brady gun bill under attack. *Chicago Tribune*, 2 December.

Greenfeld, Lawrence A., and Steven K. Smith. 1999. *American Indians and crime*. NCJ 173386. Washington, D.C.: U.S. Department of Justice, Bureau of Justice Statistics.

Hackenberg, Robert A. 1995. Joe Hill dies for your sins: Empowering minority workers in the new industrial labor force. In *Any way you cut it: Meat processing and small-town America*, edited by Donald D. Stull, Michael J. Broadway, and David Griffith. Lawrence: University Press of Kansas.

Hackenberg, Robert A., and Gary Kukulka. 1995. Industries, immigrants, and illness in the new Midwest. In *Any way you cut it: Meat processing and small-town America*, edited by Donald D. Stull, Michael J. Broadway, and David Griffith. Lawrence: University Press of Kansas.

Hall, Bob. 1995. The kill line: Facts of life, proposals for change. In *Any way you cut it: Meat processing and small-town America*, edited by Donald D. Stull, Michael J. Broadway, and David Griffith. Lawrence: University Press of Kansas.

Hastings, Don. 1985. Big bucks for poachers. *Illinois Department of Conservation: Outdoor Highlights* 13:8–11.

Heges, Stephen, Dana Hawkins, and Perry Loeb. 1996. The new jungle. *U.S. News & World Report* (September 23): 34–44.

Hobbs, Daryl. 1994. The rural context for education: Adjusting the images. In *Perspectives on violence and substance use in rural America*, edited by Stephanie M. Blaser. Oak Brook, Illinois: North Central Regional Educational Laboratory.

Howlett, Debbie. 1997. Easy-to-concoct drug often makes users turn violent. *USA Today*, 10 September.

Janofsky, Michael. 1993. Rural town ages rapidly under Saturn's influence. *New York Times*, 15 August.

Jensen, Gary E., Joseph H. Stauss, and William V. Harris. 1977. Crime, delinquency, and the American Indian. *Human Organization* 36:252–257.

Jobes, Patrick C., Elaine Crosby, Herb Weinand, and Joseph F. Donnermeyer. 1999. Crime mapping in rural Australia. In *Proceedings of Mapping the Boundaries of Australia's Criminal Justice System*. Canberra: Australian Institute of Criminology.

Johnson, Charles. 1994. Call the ag patrol. *Farm Journal* (February): 30–31.

Johnson, Eric A., and Eric H. Monkkonen, eds. 1996. *The civilization of crime: Violence in town and country since the Middle Ages*. Urbana: University of Illinois Press.

Johnson, Kenneth M., and Calvin L. Beale. 1995. The rural rebound revisited. *American Demographics* 17 (July): 46–49, 52–54.

Johnston, Lloyd D., Patrick M. O'Malley, and Jerald G. Bachman. 1998. *National survey results on drug use from the Monitoring the Future study, 1975–1997*. Rockville, Maryland: U.S. Department of Health and Human Services, National Institute on Drug Abuse.

Kilman, Scott. 1995. Iowans can handle pig smells, but this is something else: Giant hog "factories" strain inherent neighborliness of a rural community. *Wall Street Journal*, 4 May.

Kirn, Walter. 1998. Crank. *Time*, 22 June, 24–27, 29–30, 32.

Knickerbocker, Brad. 1998. U.S. fight against timber thieves. *Christian Science Monitor*, 23 March.

Lamb, David. 1996. Main Street finds gold in urban crime wave: Once-struggling rural America sees economic salvation in one of the Nation's fastest-growing, most recession-proof industries—Prisons. *Los Angeles Times*, 9 October.

Lane, Roger. 1997. *Murder in America: A history*. Columbus: Ohio State University Press.

Laub, John H. 1983. Urbanism, race, and crime. *Journal of Research in Crime and Delinquency* 20:183–198.

———. 1981. Ecological considerations in victim reporting to the police. *Journal of Criminal Justice* 9:419–430.

Law Enforcement News. 1997. Hard-boiled yeggs turn their focus to softer bank targets. 15 May.

Littrell, Donald W., and Doris P. Littrell. 1991. Civic education, rural development, and the Land Grant institutions. In *The future of rural America: Anticipating policies for constructive change*, edited by Kenneth E. Pigg. Boulder, Colorado: Westview Press.

Lyson, Thomas A. 1989. *Two sides of the Sunbelt: The growing divergence between the rural and urban South*. New York: Praeger.

Lyson, Thomas A., and William M. Falk. 1993. *Forgotten places: Uneven development in rural America*. Lawrence: University Press of Kansas.

Mann, Coramae Richey. 1993. *Unequal justice: A question of color*. Bloomington: Indiana University Press.

McCormick, John, and Paul O'Donnell. 1993. Drug wizard of Wichita: Did the chemist concoct a killer narcotic? *Newsweek*, 21 June, 32.

Miller, Martin G., Eric O. Hoiberg, and Rodney E. Ganey. 1982. Delinquency patterns of farm youth. In *Rural crime: Integrating research and prevention*, edited by Timothy J. Carter, G. Howard Phillips, Joseph F. Donnermeyer, and Todd N. Wurschmidt. Totowa, New Jersey: Allanheld, Osmun.

Moberg, David. 1996. State jobs: Economic boon or bust? *Illinois Issues* 22:14–23.

Montell, William L. 1986. *Killings: Folk justice in the upper South*. Lexington: University of Kentucky Press.

Moss, Geoffrey. 1997. Explaining the absence of violent crime among the Semai of Malaysia: Is criminological theory up to the task? *Journal of Criminal Justice* 25:177–194.

Nielsen, Marianne O., and Robert A. Silverman, eds. 1996. *Native Americans, crime and justice*. Boulder, Colorado: Westview Press.

Nisbett, Richard E., and Dov Cohen. 1996. *Culture of honor: The psychology of violence in the South*. Boulder, Colorado: Westview Press.

O'Dea, Patrick, Barbara Murphy, and Cecilia Balzer. 1997. Traffick and illegal production of drugs in rural America. In *Rural substance abuse: State of knowledge and issues*, edited by Elizabeth Robertson, Zili Sloboda, Gayle M. Boyd, Lula Beatty, and Nicholas J. Kozel. Rockville, Maryland: U.S. Department of Health and Human Services, National Institute on Drug Abuse.

Pendleton, Michael R. 1997. Looking the other way: The institutional accommodation of tree theft. *Qualitative Sociology* 20:325–340.

Perkins, Craig, and Patsy Klaus. 1996. *Criminal victimization 1994*. Report, NCJ 158022. Washington, D.C.: U.S. Department of Justice, Bureau of Justice Statistics.

Perrolle, Judith A., ed. 1993. Environmental justice. Special issue. *Social Problems* 40 (February).

Pesticide Action Network North America Update Service. 1992. California pesticide thefts on the rise. 17 September. Retrieved 2 November 1997 from the World Wide Web: http://rtk.net/E2701T598.

Peters, Victoria J., E.R. Oetting, and Ruth W. Edwards. 1992. Drug use in rural communities: An epidemiology. In *Drug use in rural American communities*, edited by Ruth W. Edwards. New York: Haworth Press.

Peterson, Peter G. 1996. *Will America grow up before it grows old?* New York: Random House.

Pimentel, David, and Marcia Pimentel. 1997. U.S. food production threatened by rapid population growth. Manuscript prepared for the Carrying Capacity Network, Washington, D.C., 30 October.

Pollan, Michael. 1997. Confessions of an American opium grower. *Harper's* (April): 35–58.

Public Employees for Environmental Responsibility and the Government Accountability Project.1997. Action alert: Timber theft group sign-on letter. 28 October. Retrieved 12 June 1998: http://www.accessone.com/gap/www/timberlet.htm.

Rachel's Hazardous Waste News #66. The new urban garbage solution: Dump it in poorer, rural areas. 29 February. Retrieved 2 November 1997 from the World Wide Web: http://rtk.net/E3391T132.

Rand, Michael R., James P. Lynch, and David Cantor. 1997. *Criminal victimization, 1973–95*. Report, NCJ 163069. Washington, D.C.: U.S. Department of Justice, Bureau of Justice Statistics.

Rephann, Terry. In press. Links between rural development and crime. *Papers in Regional Science* 78.

Ringel, Cheryl. 1997. *Criminal victimization 1996: Changes 1995–96 with trends 1993–96*. Report, NCJ 165812. Washington, D.C.: U.S. Department of Justice, Bureau of Justice Statistics.

Salamon, Sonya. 1997. Culture. In *Encyclopedia of rural America: The land and people*, edited by Gary A. Goreham. Santa Barbara: ABC–CLIO.

Sampson, Robert J. 1986. Crime in cities: The effects of formal and informal social control. In *Communities and crime*, edited by Albert J. Reiss, Jr., and Michael Tonry. Vol. 8 of *Crime and justice: A review of research*. Chicago: University of Chicago Press.

Sampson, Robert J., and Thomas C. Castellano. 1982. Economic inequality and personal victimization. *British Journal of Criminology* 22:363–385.

Sampson, Robert J., and W. Byron Groves. 1989. Community structure and crime: Testing social-disorganization theory. *American Journal of Sociology* 94:774–802.

Sampson, Robert J., Stephen W. Raudenbush, and Felton Earls. 1997. Neighborhoods and violent crime: A multilevel study of collective efficacy. *Science* 277:918–924.

Scheer, Scott D., Lynne M. Borden, and Joseph F. Donnermeyer. In press. The relationship between family factors and adolescent substance use in rural, suburban, and urban areas. *Journal of Child and Family Studies.*

Schodolski, Vincent J. 1997. Farm workers earn less than in '76, data show. *Chicago Tribune*, 12 April.

Seroka, Jim, and Seshan Subramaniam. 1991. Governing the countryside: Linking politics and administrative resources. In *The future of rural America: Anticipating policies for constructive change*, edited by Kenneth E. Pigg. Boulder, Colorado: Westview Press.

Setterberg, Fred, and Lonny Shavelson. 1993. *Toxic Nation: The fight to save our communities from chemical contamination.* New York: John Wiley & Sons.

Shichor, David. 1992. Myths and realities in prison siting. *Crime & Delinquency* 38:70–87.

Silverman, Robert A. 1996. Patterns of Native American crime. In *Native Americans, crime, and justice*, edited by Marianne O. Nielsen and Robert A. Silverman. Boulder, Colorado: Westview Press.

Smith, Brent L. 1980. Criminal victimization in rural areas. In *Criminal justice research: New models and findings*, edited by Barbara Raffael Price and Phyllis Jo Baunach. Beverly Hills: Sage Publications.

Smith, Brent L., and C. Ronald Huff. 1982. Crime in the country: The vulnerability and victimization of rural citizens. *Journal of Criminal Justice* 10:271–282.

Smith, Wes. 1996. In string of strange robberies, thieves target expensive herbicides. *Chicago Tribune*, 30 June.

St. Clair, Jeffrey, and Alexander Cockburn. 1997. Idaho's enemies: The National Guard counts environmentalists among them. *The Progressive* 61:18–20.

Statistical Analysis Center. 1985. *Farm related thefts in Iowa.* Ames, Iowa: Statistical Analysis Center, Office for Planning and Programming.

Stewart, Phil, and Gita Sitaramiah. 1997. America's heartland grapples with rise of dangerous drug. *Christian Science Monitor,* 13 November. Retrieved 13 November 1997 from the World Wide Web: http://www.csmonitor.com/todays_paper/graphical/today/us/us.2.html.

Stock, Catherine McNichol. 1996. *Rural radicals: Righteous rage in the American grain*. Ithaca, New York: Cornell University Press.

Straus, Murray, and Richard J. Gelles, eds. 1990. *Physical violence in American families: Risk factors and adaptations to violence in 8,145 families*. New Brunswick, New Jersey: Transaction Publishers.

Straus, Murray, Richard J. Gelles, and Suzanne K. Steinmetz. 1980. *Behind closed doors: Violence in the American family*. New York: Anchor Books.

Stull, Donald D., and Michael J. Broadway. 1995. Killing them softly: Work in meat-packing plants and what it does to workers. In *Any way you cut it: Meat processing and small-town America*, edited by Donald D. Stull, Michael J. Broadway, and David Griffith, Lawrence: University Press of Kansas.

Swanson, Bert E., Richard A. Cohen, and Edith P. Swanson. 1979. *Small towns and small towners: A framework for survival and growth*. Beverly Hills: Sage Publications.

Taylor, Bruce M. 1997. *Changes in criminal victimization, 1994–95*. NCJ 162032. Washington, D.C.: U.S. Department of Justice, Bureau of Justice Statistics.

Tyson, Ann Scott. 1996. Drug abuse is quiet scandal in America's countrysides. *Christian Science Monitor*, 16 September.

U.S. Bureau of the Census. 1999. POPClock. Retrieved 17 April 1999 from the World Wide Web: http://www.census.gov/main/www/popclock.html.

———. 1995. *Statistical abstract of the United States, 1995*. Washington, D.C.

———. 1993. *1990 Census of Housing: Detailed housing characteristics, Kentucky*. Report no. 1990 CH–2–19. Washington, D.C.

———. 1990. *General population characteristics, 1990*. Washington, D.C.

U.S. Department of Health and Human Services, National Center on Child Abuse and Neglect. 1988. *Study findings: National Study of the Incidence and Severity of Child Abuse and Neglect*. Washington, D.C.

———. 1981. *Study findings: National Study of the Incidence and Severity of Child Abuse and Neglect*. Washington, D.C.

U.S. Department of Justice, Federal Bureau of Investigation. 1960 through 1998. *Crime in the United States*. Uniform Crime Reports. Washington, D.C.

U.S. General Accounting Office. 1990. *Rural drug abuse: Prevalence, relation to crime, and programs*. Washington, D.C.

Van, Jon. 1997. High tech in the heartland: Intelligence and innovation counted more than technical skill when hungry entrepreneurs created new businesses in small-town Iowa. *Chicago Tribune*, 10 November.

Verde, Tom. 1998. 90's moonshiners add drugs and guns to the recipe. *New York Times*, 2 February.

Verhovek, Sam Howe. 1994. 5 rural sheriffs are taking the Brady Law to court. *New York Times*, 25 April.

Websdale, Neil. 1998. *Rural woman battering and the justice system: An ethnography*. Thousand Oaks, California: Sage Publications.

————. 1995. An ethnographic assessment of the policing of domestic violence in rural eastern Kentucky. *Social Justice* 22:102–122.

Weingarten, Paul. 1989. Profits, perils higher for today's bootleggers. *Chicago Tribune*, 14 September.

Weingarten, Paul, and James Coates. 1989. Drugs blaze new paths: Interstates, back-roads join courier system. *Chicago Tribune*, 12 September.

Weisheit, Ralph A. 1997. Marijuana. In *Encyclopedia of rural America: The land and people*, edited by Gary A. Goreham. Santa Barbara: ABC–CLIO.

————. 1993. Studying drugs in rural areas: Notes from the field. *Journal of Research in Crime and Delinquency* 30:213–232.

————. 1992. *Domestic marijuana: A neglected industry*. Westport, Connecticut: Greenwood Press.

Weisheit, Ralph A., David N. Falcone, and L. Edward Wells. 1999. *Crime and policing in rural and small-town America*. 2d ed. Prospect Heights, Illinois: Waveland Press.

Weisheit, Ralph A., and Steven T. Kernes. 1997. Future challenges: The urbanization of rural America. In *Community policing in a rural setting*, edited by Quint C. Thurman and Edmund F. McGarrell. Cincinnati: Anderson Publishing Company.

Weisheit, Ralph A., and L. Edward Wells. 1999. The future of crime in rural America. *Journal of Crime and Justice* 22 (1): 1–26.

Weisheit, Ralph A., and L. Edward Wells. 1996. Rural crime and justice: Implications for theory and research. *Crime & Delinquency* 42:379–397.

Weisheit, Ralph A., L. Edward Wells, and David N. Falcone. 1994. Community policing in small-town and rural America. *Crime & Delinquency* 40:549–567.

Wells, L. Edward, and Ralph A. Weisheit. 1998. Rural gangs: Are they a problem? Paper presented at the 1998 Annual Meeting of the American Society of Criminology, 13 November.

Williams, Christopher, ed. 1996. Environmental victims. Special issue. *Social Justice* 23 (Winter).

Wilson, William J. 1987. *The truly disadvantaged.* Chicago: University of Chicago Press.

Wolfner, Glenn D., and Richard J. Gelles. 1993. A profile of violence toward children: A national study. *Child Abuse and Neglect* 17:197–212.

Wren, Christopher S. 1997. The illegal home business: "Speed" manufacture. *New York Times*, 8 July, electronic edition. Retrieved 8 July 1997 from the World Wide Web: http://www.nytimes.com/yr/mo/day/news/national/crank-addict.html.